Idioms, Patterns, Phrasal verbs, Proverbs, Spoken English phrases, Sentences

And Much More

ENGLISH DICTIONARY

OF

IDIOMATIC EXPRESSIONS

(Up to 1000 Phrases)

Written by Muhammad Nabeel

Book Name: An English Dictionary of Idiomatic Expressions

Author: Muhammad Nabeel

Edition: 1st

Pages: 85

Date: March 2018

Author Page: www.amazon.com/author/muhammadnabeel

Content

Welcome to the English Dictionary of Idiomatic expressions.

In this book, you will learn English idioms, Phrasal verbs, Patterns, and Proverbs. Also, I have added some Spoken English phrases/Sentences that you can use in your daily life. For this, I have created a separate chapter for you.

All expressions are created in alphabetical order. So you can easily find out the meaning of the word.

I hope this book will be helpful for you. And if you have any question, please feel free to ask me anytime.

Muhammad Nabeel

Muhammadnabeel400@gmail.com

Note: Every expression might have so many definitions but I selected the only common definitions.

IDIOMS AND PHRASES

1. **(to be) At the helm:** to have a position of leadership
2. **(to be) after something:** to try to gain or get something, trying to attain something, to want something, something that is your inside and you really want,
3. **(to be) Above/beyond reproach:** to be perfect, to have no fault
4. **At someone's beck and call:** to be slave to someone
5. **Across the board:** in every area, in every aspects,
6. **At the drop of a hat:** immediately
7. **As slow as molasses:** really slow,

8. **(to be) The apple of one's eye:** to be most important thing in someone's life, to be happiest thing in someone's life
9. **(to) ace something:** to score perfectly.
10. **All that jazz:** etc..; and so on; things like that
11. **All the rage:** super popular
12. **All your ducks in a row:** well-organized
13. **(to) bite the dust:** To die
14. **(to be) bound to do something:** surely
15. **Bound to NOUN:** tied to (contract, agreement)
16. **(to) breathe over someone's shoulder:** watching very closely
17. **(to) beat around the bush:** to evade the subject,
18. **(To) brown bag it:** to bring your own lunch

19.   **Bust a move!** (1) to do something quickly, hurry up (2) to do dance very well

20.   **Busy work:** an unimportant work that boss or teacher gives you just for keeping you busy,

21.   **(to) badger someone:** to constantly ask the person question (usually same question), over and over again asking, to tell somebody to do something over and over again,

22.   **(to) beat someone to it:** to defeat,

23.   **Beyond a shadow of a doubt!** Without any doubt, absolutely sure

24.   **Bores me to tears:** extremely boring

25.   **Bawl one's eyes out:** to cry so much with actually tears

26.   **Back in the saddle:** to be back again at your work

27.   **Breakeven:** point where expenses are equal to income

28.   **Blow off steam:** to vent,

29.   **(to be) bush league:** If someone is bush league, that means, he/she is minor, low talent, beginner level, or immature. If something is bush league, that means, it is low quality or it's not so good.

30.   **Bit of a handful:** wild, difficult to control

31.   **Bragging rights:** freedom to boast one's achievement

32.   **(to) break a (bad) habit:** to stop the habit,

33.   **(to) bring in the big guns:** to bring a powerful and important person, (common in sports)

34.   **My bread and butter:** something that makes you money

35.   **In a jiffy:** very soon, in couple of minutes,

36.   **(to) crack open:** to open something just a little

37.   **(to) Cuddle:** to hug in a very loving, cute and happy way

38.   **(to) Catch a movie:** to go cinema and watch a movie,

39.   **(to) crash:** to feel extremely tired

40.   **Come to terms with (myself):** to accept the painful truth,

41.   **Cement a (relationship, friendship, deal, agreement etc.):** strong, unbreakable,

42.   **(to) come clean:** to tell the truth, confess,

43.   **Clean as a whistle:** really clean,

44.   **(to) clinch:** to secure, to grab something, (2) to secure a sports championship opportunity, to get into the final tournament,

45.   *Claim to fame:* something that makes someone unusual and important (what are you know for)

46.   **(to) dig deep:** to talk about a subject in depth, to really analyze and debate the subject

47.   **To do my darndest (darnedest):** to do my best

48.   **The devil is in the details:** something that looks simple at first look but it might contain some hidden problems,

49.   **Dead giveaway:** completely obvious, clew, certain, absolutely,

50.   **(to) ditch SOMEONE/SOMETHING:** to throw it away, to leave alone somebody,

51.   **(To) do a disservice to someone:** ill service, unhelpful service, to provide an inadequate service to someone, (2) harmful service,

52.   **(to) dazzle:** very bright and shiny like diamond, (2) to amaze and surprise,

53.   **(To) do someone:** to mimic someone (to copy someone's voice, expression, body language, style etc…)

54.   **Down in the dumps:** to be very sad and depressed,

55.   **(to) dump someone:** to break up the relationship,

56. **Drain:** deprive the energy/strength
57. **Duke it out:** Fight
58. **Down and out:** very depressed, extremely depressed,
59. **Dinner and a movie:** simple and clean date (first time)
60. **(to) draw a blank:** to have no idea right now
61. **A dope:** a stupid person,
62. **(To be) dope:** really cool/good
63. **Thing of the past:** old styled,
64. **(to) do someone's bidding:** to ask someone to do something,
65. **(to be) engaged:** to be interested,
66. **(to) eyeball something:** to look at something, to judge something, to make a guess,
67. **Eats like a bird!** eats a little bit,
68. **Eating SOMETHING like candy:** to eat lot of something at one time, continually eating as a child eat candies
69. **Easy on the eyes:** nice to look at; enjoyable to look at it (like clothing, view etc.)
70. **For shits and giggles:** just for fun,
71. **(To be) few and far between:** rare
72. **For good:** for ever
73. **(to) foot the bill:** to pay for something
74. **Fly off the handle:** to explode in anger
75. **(to) feel stifled:** to feel very frustrated,
76. **Food for thought:** something you should think about it, something we shouldn't make a quick decision,
77. **Face the music:** to look at the truth and don't lie yourself, to accept the criticism,
78. **(to) fall flat:** fail completely,
79. **First World problems:** not a series problem,

80. **(to) feign something :** to pretend, to fake being (sickness, sleeping, death)

81. **Fingers crossed:** it's a hand gesture used to wish best for someone,

82. **For starters:** for beginners, first of all,

83. **(to) freeze my butt off** super cold

84. **(to) feel a little warm:** to start feeling sick, fever,

85. **Full of himself:** love himself too much,

86. **(to) fly the coop:** to escape,

87. **For my own good:** For my own benefit

88. **Get the nod:** be approved, yes,

89. **Get the gist:** to basically understand something, basic idea of something'

90. **Give the green light:** to give the permission to do something

91. **go Dutch:** to share the cost of something like meal,

92. **Get your head out of the clouds:** be realistic, stop dreaming and wake up, come to the earth and be real

93. **Give a wide berth:** to give a lot of space

94. **Gone wild:** out of control,

95. **(to) get cold feet:** to feel uncomfortable or scared,

96. **(to) give someone a boost:** to make someone feel happy

97. **(to) get duped:** to be deceived, to be cheated, to be tricked in an evil way

98. **Go out on a limb:** to give your opinion or prediction that you really don't know, to make an assumption

99. **Go with the flow:** to follow what everybody else

does, copy the people around you,

100. **Going through a rough patch:** difficult time of period, many problems, things are not going well

101. **(to) give a holler:** call me; ask me for help, let me know and I will solve your problem, inform me if you need,

102. **(to) get a lot out of something:** to take a lot of information

103. **(to be) GIFTED:** extra special talented,

104. **Grab a nap:** to take a short sleep

105. **Give someone the benefit of the doubt:** to believe someone even though, you are not sure about that and also it sounds like lying

106. **(to) get my own way:** to do things the way I want to,

107. **#to go:** remaining, left (example: 2 to go)

108. **(to) go to bat for someone:** to support somebody by doing something (not for just saying or encourage someone),

109. **(to) get chunky:** to start to get fat

110. **(to) get the edge on someone:** to be better than someone,

111. **(to) give solace to someone:** to give something to somebody so that misery, sadness or depression can goes away of other person,

112. **Something Gets me every time:** it touches and melt my heart, it bring out the emotions,

113. **Got it bad:** to be 150% fall in love with somebody, to be massive fan of somebody, obsessed and infatuated

114. **(to) get wind of it:** to hear some rumor,

115. **(to) grill someone:** to ask someone very intense questions,

116. **(to) get your undies in a bundle / bunch:** to be anxious,

117. **Going rogue:** going wild,

118. **(to) get worked up about:** to be angry/upset about something (something is bothering you)

119. **(to) get rid of...** to throw something away, to put something in garbage,

120. **Gave up the ghost:** (something) died, broke

121. **Get the hang of:** to get used to something.

122. **Give a shout out to:** to say hello, especially in radio or in interview

123. **(to) give props to:** to give a proper respect to somebody;

124. **(to) hang your hat on (something):** (1) to believe something, (2) to proud something,

125. **Hard to beat:** Difficult to defeat, best

126. **Hit the sack:** to go to the bed for sleeping

127. **(to) hound somebody:** to harass and pester somebody, to bother somebody,

128. **(to) have the guts:** to have courage to do something, to be confident and brave,

129. **(to) have a way with:** to have a method or connection

130. **(to) hunker down:** (1) to actually get down, sit on the back of your leg like a baseball catcher; (2) defend yourself; (3) to study, to work hard, to get series, to really focus, to concentrate,

131. **(to) have no say:** to have no power, to have no authority, to have no influence,

132. **Head over heels:** to be in love

133. **Holy crap!** Oh my God, What the, really, Wow!

134. **(to) have a penchant for:** to have a strong desire for something (especially for food)

135. **Honest to a fault:** too much honest,

136. **(to) hang in the balance:** if something is hanging in the balance, it means, you are waiting for result. And you don't know what will happen. It depends' on somebody else's decision.

137. **(to) horse around:** to play like a children,

138. **(to) have no call to do something:** to not have right/permission to do something,

139. **To have a chip on your shoulder:** to be a very angry (long time anger)

140. **Head in the sand:** to ignore some obvious fact, (there is some obvious truth that you don't want to see and hear it)

141. **(to be) in denial:** to ignore the harshness or terrible fact, to not accept the reality

142. **In my book:** In my opinion,

143. **bumpy ride:** dangerous situation, difficult time,

144. **In the shade:** in the shadow, place that protected you from the intense sun rays like trees,

145. **In its clutches:** to grab something (not normal grabbing, it is tight grabbing), holding on very tightly,

146. **(to be) in THE moment:** give full attention with all of your senses,

147. **(to be) in its infancy:** to be just a baby plan that is still growing

148. **In a heartbeat:** to do something very quickly, instantly, without thinking,

149. **In a rut:** To have same boring routines everybody. And there is no changing in life.

150. **In a nutshell:** in short and simple words,

151. **In a huff:** angrily,

152. **Itching to do something:** really wanting to do something,

153.   **In the limelight:** If some news/subject is in the limelight that means, everybody is talking about this new in these days. If a person is in the limelight, that means, he is superstar, so everybody can see him.

154.   **(to be) in the cards:** in the fate, in the star, in the destiny,

155.   **In broad daylight:** in complete middle of the afternoon (when sun is shining)

156.   **In tip-top shape:** best, excellent,

157.   **In a roundabout way:** indirectly,

158.   **Jump the shark:** something (film, television show) is no longer super popular,

159.   **(to) josh someone:** to tease, joke around,

160.   **Knock on wood:** said in order to avoid bad luck

161.   **(to) keep someone on their toes::** to force someone to concentrate, to make someone be alert.

162.   **(to) kill two birds with one stone:** to get two things done in one stroke,

163.   **(to) kick start something:** to get a lot of energy and power to get something moving, (we use it in business); to start fresh and strong,

164.   **(that work) Kicked my behind:** that work was really tiring and exhausting.

165.   **(to) lack something:** to not have enough of something, something is insufficient,

166.   **A little too strange:** not good but in middle

167.   (1) very: positive meaning (2) too: negative (3) a little too: middle both of them

168.   **(to) leg it:** to walk, run very quickly,

169.   **To lose one's cool:** To become very angry

170.   **(to) lose one's bearings:** to lose direction (2)to lose focus and concentration,

171.   **The lesser of two evils:** the less unpleasant of two undesirable choices,

172.   **(To be) loaded:** (1) to be rich (2) completely drunk

173.   **My diet:** my food

174.   **(to) make ends meet:** Barely earn enough money to survive, live on the edge of poverty

175.   **My two cents:** my humble opinion

176.   **(to) move mountains:** to achieve apparently impossible thing,

177.   **Man the grill:** to operate something, to handle something,

178.   **(to) milk it:** to try to take too much advantage over something,

179.   **Make a pitch:** to promote something,

180.   **Music to my ears:** if something is music to your ears, that means, you love to hear this; you really like that thing. For example, *"download this book free."* Is that music to your ears?

181.   **(to) make or break:** sometimes, you do something that require a lot of money, all of our energy or risking everything. And if you fail, your future would break; and if you get success, you future would be bright. This is the idea.

182.   **Meant to be:** For example, we were meant to be. That means, we were destiny to be. The God, fate, or universe eventually was going to put us together and keep us together.

183.   **Nuke it:** to reheat something in microwave oven.

184.   **Not nearly enough:** Not enough (emphasizing)

185.   **Nothing but the best:** only the best,

186.   **(to) nip it in the bud:** to stop something from (bad) happing or growing to big.

187.   **Never delivers:** If somebody makes a promise, but they never fulfill their promise, then we can say *"he never delivers"*

188.   **No less (so) than:** A and B are same

189.   **Oversleep:** to wake up late

190.   **On the edge:** on the risky/dangerous situation

191.   **Ordering take-out:** Ordering food from outside like restaurant

192.   **Out of the blue:** Suddenly, not anticipated

193.   **On and off...off and on:** occasionally, sometime, not regularly,

194.   **On the rocks:** relationship that is not healthy and has problems (2) some drinks with ice

195.   **On a health kick:** to really concentrate on health

196.   **(to be) outta sorts:** to be angry, to be feel little frustrated (2) to be confused, to be stressed,

197.   **On the sly:** secretly, to do something sneakily,

198.   **(to be) on thin ice:** to be in very dangerous situation

199.   **(to be) on the level with someone:** to be straightforward with someone, being honest,

200.   **On the dole:** receiving government support,

201.   **On so many levels:** in so many different ways or aspects,

202.   **(to) offset:** to make something balance

203.   **On the off chance:** By chance

204.   **out of whack:** not working properly, out of order

205.   **(to be) over someone:** to no longer have emotions (especially in relationship)

206. **Out in the bush:** this expression is opposite of "in the city"

207. **A pain in the neck:** Something that makes you annoying is called a pain in the neck

208. **Pushover:** someone who is very easy to overcome or influence by someone,

209. **Pushing up daisies:** dead

210. **Pretty beat:** tired,

211. **(to) put something into perspective:** to compare with something similar to give a clear and accurate idea,

212. **(to) pick someone's brain:** to ask somebody for their expert opinion,

213. **(to) put a smile on my face:** makes me happy

214. **(to) put it bluntly:** to be very honest (with your opinion/words/comments, even though you might hurt or angry other person)

215. **(to) put lipstick on a pig:** something is really bad but we try to make it really nice; it is the same as putting lipstick on a pig.

216. **Put a dent into something:** to reduce an amount of something (especially work)

217. **(to) put the kibosh on something:** to stop something from happening or continuing,

218. **Put a crimp in my plan:** cause problem, to interfere with the plan

219. **(to) pull the wool over someone's eyes:** to deceive somebody by making them confused and blind,

220.   **(to) pull the plug:** to shut down,

221.   **(to) pigeonhole someone:** to judge someone based on stereotype,

222.   **Put some hair on your chest:** to become strong,

223.   **(to) pull your weight:** to do a work what you are supposed to do, to be responsible for your work

224.   **(to) pay top dollar:** to pay a lot of money,

225.   **(To) rain on someone's parade:** to spoil someone's plan

226.   **(to) run ragged:** to be super, ultra, extremely busy and you are getting really tired

227.   **Right off the bat:** immediately, without hesitation,

228.   **(to) rattle someone:** to scare someone, to upset someone, to confuse someone, to nerves someone,

229.   **Raise the roof:** to get really loud and excited,

230.   **Run of the mill:** just regular and nothing special,

231.   **(To) Steal my thunder:** to steal my applause, to steal my day or event.

232.   **Sticks out like a sore thumb:** it is opposite of "to blend in"

233.   **Stupid is as stupid does:** somebody who is not stupid because of their mental ability but he does stupid thing, then we can use this expression.

234.   **Starting is half the battle:** starting is so difficult

235.   **I'm sticking to my guns:** I am not going to change mind what I believe or opinion,

236.   **Straight and narrow:** to live by the rules (moral principles)

237.   **Say something out in the open:** to say something that is private or personal,

238. **(to) sweep SMT under the rug:** hide the some personal information

239. **Slip through the cracks:** escape,

240. **(to) sweep someone off his/her feet:** to make someone fell in love with you

241. **Stoop so low as to:** to be overly humble; to actually degrade yourself, (2) go down to really low level morality, to be low person, to be disgusting person, to do something evil to somebody

242. **Spick and span:** perfectly clean

243. **Standing in my way:** something is blocking me

244. **Stay ahead of the game:** to have an advantage for some competitive situation

245. **(to) stifle something:** to control some person, to restrain somebody, to not allow somebody to breath, to suffocate somebody,

246. **Spring forward, fall back!** In the spring, we move our clock forward 1 hour, and in the fall (in the autumn) we move our clock back 1 hour.

247. **Save my spot!** Save my place

248. **A solid background in:** strong and tight background

249. **(to) solidify something:** to make something solid, to make strong and best

250. **(to be) slapped with a fine:** if you get a fine or some sort of penalty then you can say *'I got slapped with fine."* I got slapped with penalty.

251. **Sound asleep:** sleeping very deeply,

252. **A sub / to sub for:** to substitute,

253. **A show of hands:** display hands,

254. **Skip the middleman:** idea of this expression is; if you buy a food from former, it's going to be cheaper than buying food at the grocery store. The store is the middle man.

255. **Smack-dab in the middle:** directly, precisely,

256. **My soul mate:** unusually close to some person, your habit and likes are same with that person, perfectly match with other person,

257. **(to) split the difference:** to compromise and agree on something,

258. *Shoot myself in the foot:* Idea is, you are trying to make a situation better, but you're actually making the situation worst.

259. **(She is) HIGH MAINTENANCE (this expression is for women):** picky person, demanding person,

260. **(to be) shrouded in mystery:** covered in mystery,

261. **Shook me to my core:** it shocked me

262. **Taking forever:** taking a long time

263. **(to) Tweak it!** to change a little bit.

264. **Take it with a grain of salt:** In this expression, 'To take it with a grain of salt' it may refer to promise, insult, threat etc.

265. **Trash it:** to destroy something (2) to throw something away

266. **(to) throw a party:** to have a party,

267. **The tide has turned against:** something is not good for me; it is not in my favor,

268. **A token something:** typical,

269. **Take a dump:** to go to the bathroom

270. **Take a dip:** to get into the swimming pool,

271. **(to) throw in the towel:** to give up, to surrender, to stop

272. **Taken aback:** to be very surprised, shocked (negative way - So not happy about news)

273. **(to) talk a mile a minute:** to talk really fast,

274. **(to) take part:** to participate, to join,

275. **(to) take APART (two definitions!):** (1) to disassemble something, (2) to analyze, to study very carefully,

276. **(to) take something by storm:** to go someplace and everybody so excited, crazy and happy,

277. **Travel halfway around the world to :** want to really to do something, would do everything to do something (for example: I would travel halfway around the world to meet that girl)

278. **(to) throw a temper tantrum:** kids are temper tantrum. If they ask to you buy something and you don't do that, they would be crazy and will cry.

279. **Things that make you go hmm:** things that make you think, things that make you wonder

280. **(to) take the high road:** to make your decision based on moral, to take the moral route, to do right thing.

281. **(to) Turn over a new leaf:** to turn a page on a book (2) change your life, start a new life

282. **(to be) taken for a ride:** For example, *"You took me for a ride."* That means, you deceived me; you used me;

283. **(to) take it in stride:** something bad happened but you don't allow it effective

284. **Tough as nails::** person who can't be persuaded, physically and emotionally strong,

285. **Take the edge off:** reduce the intensity of something unpleasant

286. **Take one for the team:** accept something negative that the team wins

287. **(to) talk trash/smack:** to say something not nice, to say mean things

288. **That's the way the cookie crumbles:** that's the reality, life isn't perfect,

289. **(to) throw a softball:** to give someone a very easy question,

290. **Thanks for the heads up:** thank you for telling me, thanks for that information,

291. **Out in the sticks:** far in the country

292. **Up and about:** recovered from an illness, (2) awake

293. **(to) upstage someone:** to do better then somebody else, but… somebody else is important person like your boss, a star or a leader; somebody else that everybody loves.

294. **(to be) under the weather:** to be sick, to not feeling well,

295. **Up in the air:** something is undecided,

296. **Up to speed:** to have studied all of material, to have read all the information,

297. **Wet behind the ears:** I am wet behind the ears. That means, I am still learning how to do something. I am immature. I still have to do lot of work for becoming proficient.

298. **Wrapped around someone's finger:** to control someone completely,

299. **(to be) watered-down:** not strong and powerful, not full version

300. **(to be) way off (the) mark:** completely miss the target

301.

EXPRESSIONS

DAILY ENGLISH IDIOMATIC SENTENCES

1 - **Are you done yet?** Are you finished yet? Are you completed yet?

2 - **I beg to differ:** Please let me tell you my different thought, I disagree with you,

3 - **Beats me:** I don't know

4 - **Bite me!** Go to the hell, get out of here, shut up and leave me alone, don't ask me, don't bother me,

5 - **Back at you!** You too,

6 - **Back in my heyday:** back when I was young and fresh,

7 - **Back off:** get away, do not get close, don't touch my stuff,

8 - **My brain's fried:** my brain is not functioning, my brain is dying,

9 - **Clear your head:** get rid of the stress,

10 - **Count your blessings:** remember your good fortune/luck,

11 - **Close, but no cigar:** you are almost correct but not 100% right,

12 - **Can you back it up?** Do you have any proof, show me,

13 - **Copy that:** okay, I understand, I got it,

13 - **Cut me some slack:** don't worry and give me a break/freedom and trust me,

14 - **Cry me a river:** stop complaining me, shut up

14 - **Cut to the chase:** don't tell the useless stuff and come to the point

14 – It's crunch time: It's time to really work hard,

15 - Don't sweat it! Don't worry about it and just relax, don't stress out,

16 - Damned if I do, damned if I don't! Whatever I do it is not good

17 - I'm in deep doo doo. I am in trouble; I have a big problem

18 - It doesn't measure up. It is good but it is not standard, it is not as good,

19 - Don't jump the gun: don't start too soon; don't be hasty; wait

20 - Don't quote me on that: I am not exactly sure, it might be wrong (2) don't tell anyone that I said

21 - Don't knock it 'til you try it! Don't criticize before you try, don't say anything bad about it until you try it,

22 -it doesn't cut it: it doesn't meet standard, it's not good enough

23 - Don't get fresh with me: don't disrespect with me, show your respect,

24 - Do the math! Figure out it, (2) of course! Are you idiot? Figure it out yourself,

26 - Do not pass GO. Do not collect $200: you'll lose, nothing you'll get

27 - Go away! Get out, leave me alone, quit bothering me,

28 - Go figure! Wow, Amazing, surprising, it doesn't make really sense

29 - Grow up! Be mature; don't act like a little boy,

30 - Give me some feedback: Give me your opinion,

31 - I got a beef with you: I have a complaint with you, I am very angry at you

32 - It gives me a complex: it makes me feel inferior,

33 - Get the vote out! Go there and vote,

34 - Go for it: try and do it,

35 - Golly! Wow, oh my God, really

36 - Go big or go home: do your best, do everything for it,

37 - Good on you! Good for you, congratulation,

38 - Give it a shot: try it, go for it, (you have nothing to lose, so try it)

39 - Here you go. VS There you go, Here/there you are

If you give something to somebody, you can use this expression. For example, you works in a restaurant as a waiter. So you bring a hamburger for a customer and say *"here you go"* Or *"here you are"*

All these expressions have same meaning with slightly difference.

40 - How do you like them apples-!!

I am better or clever than you, you thought I can't do it but I did it,

41 - How does that strike you? What is your first impression/reaction?

42 - He's OFF: he is not working today,

43 - He's in: he is working today.

44 - He can hold his own:

If somebody drinks a lot of alcohol, but he is ok. Then we can say *"he can hold his own."* Some people can't drink a lot.

45 - I have a condition

My friend likes dark chocolate but he doesn't like dairy food like milk, curd, or milk chocolate.

So one day, he went to the store, and he looks some chocolate. He asked him, *"is that milk chocolate or dark?"* The person said *"dark chocolate"*

So my friend bought and eat them. 30 minutes later, another person told him *"it was milk chocolate"*

So when he found the truth, he screamed *"oh my God,"* and instantly, he runs to the bathroom. There was explosion. My friend has a condition. That means, he has medical problem/ allergic.

So he should say to the person. *"I have milk condition; is this dark chocolate or milk chocolate."*

Then the other person knows that he has medical problem which might be horrible.

47 - He who smelt it dealt it: the person who smell the fart first, is the person who farted

48 - Have at it! Go ahead, try it, do it,

49 - Have a go! Give it try, try it once, go for it,

50 - I'm gonna kick back: I'm gonna relax

51 - I couldn't help it: I couldn't control myself; I couldn't stop myself

52 - I am broke: I have no money,

54 - I could not have said it better: what you said is perfect; you describe situation perfectly

55 - It doesn't agree with me. It doesn't match me, it doesn't suite me, I don't like it,

56 - It's all Greek to me! I don't understand it

57 - It'll never fly: it will never be successful, it won't succeed

58 - It's raining with cats and dogs: it's raining with a large & huge amount, heavy rain,

59 - I've been out of it

When you are feeling tired and exhausted, then you can use this expression.

60 - I can't thank you enough! I am very thankful to you.

61 - I'm good: _No thank you,

62 - It don't mean jack! It's meaningless, it doesn't mean anything, (2) it is a lie,

63 - I can't make head nor tail: I can't understand, I can't distinguish,

64 - I'm sitting on it

I have a good idea, but it is still baby or egg. So I want to use this good idea, but not yet.

65 - I feel less and less so

You are confident on some point, but now confident is starting to disappear. Before that, you were very confident, but now you are not very confident. You can say "*I feel less and less so*"

66 - It ain't over 'til it's over! I'm not finished until everything is complete, I will continue...

67 - I second that! I agree (what you said)

68 - Kick it up a notch: increase it (to increase volume, energy etc...)

69 - Keep it down! Keep the noise down; keep the volume down;

70 - Keep them coming! Continue to asking me

71 - Keep it together: relax, keep calm, don't lose your emotion, don't cry, don't be scare

72 - Knock yourself out (American meaning): help yourself, feel free, go for it and I give you permission.

73 - Keep your nose clean: don't get into trouble; don't do unethical/illegal things

74 - Kirk, out: Good bye,

76 - I had a long week: I had a difficult, tiring, exhausting or stressful week

76 - it's Harder than you think: it's more difficult than you expected,

76 - I changed my mind.

It means that you decided to do something but later; you don't want to do that. You changed your mind.

77 - Look no further: don't look anymore (because your looking is done; you found it); no more question

77 - Label me: think of me as, put me into category,

78 - Leave no stone unturned: look everywhere, search everywhere

79 - Lock, stock and barrel everything,

80 - Lean on me: grab me when you feel difficulties, rely on me

81 - Lay it on me! Tell me whatever is bothering you,

82 - Lucky me: I am so lucky (We use this expression in sarcastic situation when you are unlucky)

83 - Let it go: stop thinking about it, stop worrying about it, forget about it,

84 - Live it up: improve your living lifestyle (of course is expensive), enjoy oneself, live a king, spend time an extremely enjoyable way

this like in

85 - Lo and behold: surprising but not super surprising,

86 - My hat's off to you

We use this expression to say congratulation or great; and also this expression shows respect to another person.

For example, if you say to me that your English is improving because of my book; then I would say to you *"my hat's off to you."* That means, congratulation.

87 - My dogs are barking! My feet are sour; I am tired,

88 - Man it up! Be a man; don't be a baby

89 - He's mature for his age. He is young but he is intellectually/ emotionally mature

90 - I have made in the shade: My life is perfect; everything is wonderful, I have lots of money and I have very nice life.

91 - More power to you! That's great, I love to hear that

92 - Mum's the word: don't say anything, don't tell anybody,

93 - My lips are sealed: I won't tell anything what you know, your secret is safe with me,

94 - I misspoke: I said wrong word, I didn't mean to say that

95 - My plate is full: I am very busy, I have so many things to do

96 - He is my brother from another mother: we are best friend

98 - My heart isn't in it...

I don't feel interested in it.

For example, You want to study English, but your heart isn't it. That means, mentally, you want to study English, but you are not feeling motivated. You don't have the passion.

99 - No ifs, ands or buts! No excuses

100 - The News knocked my socks off! It totally shocked me; I couldn't believe it

101 - It's not carved in stone: it's not absolute, it's not principal, it's not series stuff,

102 - No pun intended: you made a pun unintentionally

103 - No strings attached: it's completely free,

105 - Never felt (some feeling): never felt happier; never felt sadder; are the most common example of this expression.

If you say never felt happier; that means, you are very happy today and you have never been happy in the past like today.

107 - One step forward, two steps back: doing worst (feeling)

108 - Oh boy! oh my goodness, this is not very good, oh no,

109 - Pick your poison

Actually we use this expression to choose our alcohol or some unhealthy food. So you are at alcohol bar and looking at the Manu and the person ask you *"pick your poison."*

110 - Put some elbow into it: use or put some extra power into it, use your muscles,

111 - Pipe down: shut up

112 - Put your best foot forward: make a good impression, be positive and have natural smile

113 - Pass it on/along: continue to pass something, continue to spread information, secret or object; share it

114 - I'm rather upset

<u>**Meaning:**</u> Actual meaning of word **'rather'** is   *'a little, tiny'*

But here it's mean   *'Extremely upset/angry or frustrated'*

115 - Raise your glass: cheers,

116 - I slept in: I woke up naturally

117 - Suit yourself: be good to be yourself;

you like it but I don't like it

118 - It spoke to me

<u>Meaning:</u> Something was saying something to me; they were talking to me; they were influencing to me; it has special meaning for me.

<u>Explanation:</u> This painting spoke to me. My book spoke to me; my shirt, shoes, song, pillow, spoke to me. They all things were talking to me and I could not ignore.

119 - Stay on my tail! follow me closely, stay right behind me, don' lose sight of me

120 - I'm stumped: I don't know how to solve the problems; I can't work on problems,

121 - Save it for a rainy day: save money for difficult time

122 - Same to you!

For example you says to me *"happy new year"*

I would say *"same to you"*

That means, I have same feeling for you

123 - Sit tight: sit down and don't move; be patient just wait;

124 - Sounds about right: yes, I think that is correct, I think so, that's probably right,

125 - Short and sweet

For example, how was the movie? Short and sweet. That means, it was short and it didn't require much time

126 - You are smarter than you look

You looks stupid but actually you are very intelligent,

127 - The sky's the limit! There is no limit,

128 - That's pure nonsense. It doesn't make any sense; that is absolutely not true

129 - That hits the spot!

if you are really thirsty or hungry for something and after finishing, you can say "that hits the spot". And it means; that was delicious and good. That is exactly what is required.

130 - That figures: I understand, I am not surprised,

130 - Take a long walk off a short pier…

<u>Meaning</u>: go into the river and don't come back (if you are anger on somebody you can use this. But this is not very nice expression.

131 - Take cover: protect yourself,

132 - Tell me about it: I know

133 - Take a crack at it: give it a try, have a go,

134 - That ship has sailed: that opportunity has gone, it's not coming back, forget about it

135 - There's nothing to it: it's easy

136 - Use your noggin: use your head, think about and solve the problem, use your intellect,

137 - Viewer discretion is advised

you might not want to watch this video, (because there could be violence, bad language, disgusting, etc…)

138 - What do you do for a living?

What is your job? How do you make money? How do you earn money?

139 - My knee went out

If your knee is hurt and you did not break your knee. It's just twisted, stretched or strain, and your knee is not working properly, then you can use this expression. *"My knee went out."*

When you get older, many things goes out. Maybe, after every six months, your back went out; your ankle went out; your elbow went out.

140 - What's up this weekend?

Do you have any plans this weekend? Is anything happening this weekend?

141 - What purpose does it serve?

What is it used for? What is its function?

142 - What the heck is wrong with you?

what is your problem?

143 - Who are you- Einstein

Explanation: It has two meaning negative & positive. If someone is very smart & intelligent, than we say to him.

In negative meaning; if you have a friend that saying something and becoming very smart; He knows everything, and that's making you crazy. So you say *"Who are you? Einstein"*

And in a positive situation, when somebody says something really intelligent, you can use this expression.

144 - What do you think?

of course, what a stupid question, why are you asking this, you know that

145 - What's your approach?

what is your strategy, how would you handle the situation

146 - What's all the racket?

what is all that noise, why is it loud outside

147 - What's all the fuss about?

what's all the racket? (similar expression)

148 - What for: why

149 - What have you been up to?

What have you been doing?

150 - When pigs fly

that's impossible,

151 - What's your take?

what is your opinion?

152 - What is he to you?

what is your opinion about him (2) what is your relationship with him?

153 - What keeps you up at night?

why haven't you able to sleep tonight; is there something bothering/worrying you

154 - Who's your money on?

who do you think would win? (If you going to do bet)

155 - What the

Actually we are missing word; what the hell; what the hack. You are angry and you want to say what's going on.

156 - Will do

ok, I will do it,

157 - What gives?

what's problem; what's the reason you did that; why did you do it;

158 - Watch your step!

be careful where you are stepping

159 - What a joke (in negative meaning not funny)

oh my God and I can't believe that; that is terrible and ridicules; what is that;

160 - Whatever floats your boat

whatever makes you happy; You can do what you want,

161 - When the rooster crows

I get up early in the morning when the rooster/cock crows.

162 - Wait up!

completely stop and wait for me

163 - What's the rush?

what's the hurry, why do you need to be so quick, let's relax

164 - What do you got?

What do you have?

165 - What's the drill?

what is the proper procedure, what am I supposed to do,

166 - What good is it?

what is the use?

167 - You name it: you decide, it's up to you,

168 - Yes siree, Bob! absolutely,

169 - Your wish is my command^^

absolutely, yes I will do it for you.

170 - You're too GOOD for your own good! (Negative meaning)

it's not good for you,

171 - You know your Greeks!

Explanation: We use this expression, when we find a person specialist in something. For example, you go to the restaurant with your friend and order a chocolate cake. And after seeing the cake, your friend instantly says

"This cake has 75% chocolate."

"Wow! You know your chocolate!" (you surprise and says)

172 - You know what they say

Meaning: you know the common saying,

Explanation: For example, Yesterday, I started exercising. And today, my all body is tired, and I don't want to exercise. So I say to my friend *"oh john, my muscles are killing me. I am not going to exercise anymore"*

Then, my friend would say *"Nabeel, you know what they say"*

And I would understand, 'No pain no gain.'

173 - You bet (2 meanings!)

no problem, you're welcome, my pleasure, (2) sure, I will,

174 - You scratch my back, I'll scratch yours

if you help me, I will help you

175 – You nailed it…you killed it: it was perfect,

175 - Yikes (interjection)

<u>Explanation:</u> we say this when we are scared or when we surprise/shocked.

176 - Zip it: be quiet, shut up,

177 – Zilch: No, none, nothing

PROVERBS

1 - Apple doesn't fall far from the tree:

Like father/son/daughter son, the son is not very different from his father, kids are like their parents,

2 – All that glitters is not gold:

Everything that looks attractive and precious, cannot be reliable.

3 - Better safe than sorry

It's wise to be careful than to be hasty and so do something you may later regret. For example, it's cloudy day, but better safe than sorry. So make sure take an umbrella. It might be rain.

4 - Beggars can't be choosers

A person who has no other options must be gratified with what is offered. For example,

If a homeless guy goes to the burger shop and asks for it, than shopkeeper gives a regular burger. And homeless guy says "no, not this burger, I need other burger"

And then shopkeeper says "are you crazy? Beggars can't be choosers; get out of here"

5 - Birds of a feather flock together.

People like to spend time with those who have same interest.

6 - Denial ain't just a river in Egypt

that person is in denial,

7 - Don't bite the hand that feeds you.

If someone is helping you or paying you, don't act badly and be careful not to make them angry.

8 - The early bird gets the worm

wake up early and you will get success,

9 - Fortune favors the bold.

People who boldly go after what they want are more successful than people who try to live safely.

10 - Give him an inch and he'll take a mile

we use this expression to describe a very greedy person. If you give him a very tiny opportunity or little advantage; he will take more; he will take too much.

11 - Haters gonna hate

people who hate you (who are jealous with you), are going to hate you no matter what you do

12 - Hope for the best, but prepare for the worst.

Be optimistic, but always be prepared for difficult time, because bad things might happens in any time.

13 - Keep your friends close and your enemies closer.

Always, be closer with your enemies than friends, so you can know if they are going to harm you.

14 - No man is an island.

No one can live completely independently. Everybody needs help from other people.

15 - Out of sight, out of mind

Meaning: if you can't see it you don't think about it; you soon forget people or things that are no longer visible or present.

Explanation: For example, if you want to lose weight but you love cookies. So you need to get rid of cookies. Out of sight, out of mind. That means, if you don't have cookies in your house, you are not going to think about it.

16 - The proof of the pudding is in the eating

it looks good, it probably taste good. But if you want to proof, you need to eat it. When you eat it, than you know whether it tasty or not. The real value of something is only judged by practical experience.

17 - The pen is mightier than the sword.

Trying to persuade people with words and ideas is more powerful than trying to force people to do something.

18 - People who live in glass houses should not throw stones.

If you're not perfect, do not criticize others.

19 - A picture is worth a thousand words.

A complex idea can be conveyed with just a single Picture. And it is much better than a lot of written words.

20 - The squeaky wheel gets the grease.

If you complain about something, you can get better service. But if you wait patiently, no one will help you.

21 - Two wrongs don't make a right.

If somebody has done something bad with you and after that, you try to get revenge, then that will only make things worse.

22 - There's no such thing as a free lunch.

It is not possible to get something for free, because every free thing have also hidden cost.

23 - There's no place like home.

Your home is the best place of all places.

24 - There's More than one way to skin a cat

There's more than one way to do something, there's several ways to succeed,

25 - Tit for tat

ideas is that; if you hit me I will hit you. If you say something bad me, I will say you bad.

26 - A watched pot never boils.

If you are watching closely; if you are waiting for something to happen, Time will pass very slowly.

27 - When the going gets tough, the tough get going.

Stronger people never give up when they have difficult time and challenges. They just work harder.

28 - a wolf in lamb's clothing:

A person who seems to be friendly and good but in fact, he is not good. He is hostile.

29 - You reap what you sow

Meaning: What you will do right now, that would you get; (if you will do bad things then bad things will happen and if you do good things then good things will happen to you)

If you will now work hard, after few times, you will get succeed

30 - You snooze, you lose

Meaning: (*snooze mean sleep*), if you sleep you will lose,

Explanation: For example, if you are not paying attention; if you are daydreaming and not focusing, than you would lose the opportunity; you would lose the chance to be successful. You snooze, you lose!

31 - You can lead a horse to water... but you can't make it drink

You can give someone an opportunity but you can't force them to take an advantage of it,

You can show you the truth; you can guide someone, but you can't make someone to do something.

That person is the only person, who can do that.

32 - You can't make an omelet without breaking a few eggs.

You can never achieve your desired object without any harm.

PATTERNS

1 - All I gotta do is...

All I need to do is; I only need to do this

2 - Alls I need is...

the only thing I need is,

3 - A considered B:

A is a thought to be B; is the legal definition of A is B

4 - A trumps B: A defeats B, A is better than B, A is more powerful than B,

5 - Because of ...

we use it as an excuse. Because of something, I couldn't do.... something

6 – Binge + VERB ing

to completely in, with all your time, too much,

7 - Before my time...

before my generation, before I was born

8 - But no---

For example, I have to attend an online conference with my teacher at 1:00 pm. But at that time, I got some internet connection problems and I couldn't attend the conference. So I can say like that *"I could have been attending a conference, but no..."*

So idea is that, something should've happened, but because of some silly and stupid problem, it couldn't happen.

9 – Something… is a big plus:

Something is extra excellent, extra good,

10 – I beside myself in…

we use this, when we are shocked or surprised, and our emotions are so strong.

For example, I beside myself in grief. That means, I was so sad; I heard something and I was speechless. I didn't know what to say.

Other examples are; I beside myself in anger. I beside myself in frustration. I beside myself in happiness.

12 - (Something)… is it!

Something is Best or perfect,

13 - …Can't help but do… something

Nothing can stop from something,

14 - (I was) conned into VERB ing

to be tricked, to be deceived,

15 – Something…. is dogging me

Something is bothering me

16 - I'm finna – (I am fixing to)

to begin or start, planning, going to, intending to

17 - Did you get out something?

Get out means 'go'. The pattern is 'did you get out something?'

For example, did you get out shopping last night; did you get out dancing last night? That means, did you go shopping or dancing last night?

18 - My gut tells me...

I have a feeling inside (not emotional feeling, it's just guess), my instincts tell me.

19 - Give credit where credit is due ....

thank you very much but I also want to say thank you to that person; Don't give me all credit, give credit to this person too,

20 - I got a bad feeling about...

It means; for some reason, I think something that is going to happen, will not be good.

For example, I have a job interview. But you I a bad feeling. For some reason, I think something is not good; I might be fail.

21 - "A" is a household name or thing!

Everybody knows it

22 - I'm into... (Something)

I am very interested in (something)

23 - It will all come down to...

most important thing will be, it will dependent on (factor)

24 - If I were in your shoes... (If I were you...)

if I could see the world in your perspective

25 - I've been meaning to tell you...

I suppose to tell you but I forgot, I wanted to tell you but I forgot

26 - I like them… (PLURAL!)

When we want to emphasize, then we say this. For example, I like them videos. I like them books. It means I like your videos or I like your books.

Notice, this expression is grammatically incorrect, but everybody in America has this as an expression.

27 - I just don't happen to…

yes, but not this; yes, but not now

28 - I have a hankering for…

I want… (something)

29 - I can't shake… (something)

I can't get rid of (something like sad feeling)

30 - I'm off out…. TIME

For example, I am off out shopping Saturday. It means; I'm off. I am not working and I am not be at home. I will be out shopping.

31 - I can live with some….

I can tolerate with some

32 - I need to get out more--

For example, I mostly lived inside and I don't go anywhere, so I need to get out more. That means, I need to go to the many places like mountain. I need to go to the movies. Idea is that, I am missing something cultural.

33 - I could use (something to drink/eat)

<u>Meaning</u>: I want to have (in special meaning)

<u>Explanation</u>: Many people drinks coffee because they just like coffee. But I drink coffee because I need coffee. After drinking coffee, I become fresh and I am be able to write books. So in this case, I would say, *"I could use a coffee."* That means, I want to have coffee.

34 - I owe it all to…. somebody

I need to say thanks to somebody;

because of somebody; thanks to somebody,

35 - (Noun) is not all that (adjective)

For example, Mic is not all that handsome. That means, Mic is a little handsome. He is not very handsome.

36 - I'm looking into VERB (ing)

<u>Meaning:</u> I am thinking about

<u>Explanation:</u> For example, I am looking into traveling. I am looking into buying a new computer.

37 - (to) mold A into B

to shape or design something into something

38 – Something….is perfect mix of A and B

<u>Meaning:</u> perfect combination, perfect blend

39 (Place)…. is a dump!

Meaning: terrible place (not a nice place, a dirty place)

Explanation: we use this expression to describe the apartment or restaurant.

40 - The Powers that be….

Meaning: behind the scene,

41 - So much for… (a particle thing)

Meaning: useless, what a waste,

42 - Thanks to….

Explanation: we have studied 'because of' and we've used it as an excuse. But this expression is kind of its opposite. It is used in positive situation.

Thanks to you, I smile every day.

Thanks to my washing machine, I've clean clothes.

Thanks to this lotion, I look young

43 - There needs to be….

Meaning: (something is) required, necessary

Explanation: How we use this pattern in sentence? Here is the examples;

There needs to be more focus; there needs to be more sugar; there needs to be more time etc…

44 - (Is not) up to task

Explanation: my golf is not up to the task; my math is not up to the task and it means my golf & math used to be good a long time ago, but now

I haven't studied the math. So it's not that good. Maybe I shouldn't help to anybody in math.

45 - (to have something) Under my belt

Meaning: to have experience,

46 - And whatnot

this & that, whatever, etc., other things like that,

47 - When it comes to….

regarding, when we talk about, when we think about,

48 - What do you say we…

Let's do something, how about

49 - We might as well do….

I should do something but actually I don't want to (There is not energy and enthusiasm for doing something,)

Explanation: For example, after writing, I might as well do watch movie. That means, I don't want to watch a movie but I should watch. There is not energy or enthusiasm.

50 - You and me...me and you...You and I...

Meaning: 'you and I' is subject. 'You and me' is an object

Explanation: You and I went to the store. (Subject)

He bought you and me a candy bar. (Object)

PHRASAL VERBS

1. **All tied up:** really busy; to not have any time
2. **(to be) awash in:** to have a lot of something, to be drowning in something
3. **(to feel) Boxed in:** to feel tight; to feel like you can't escape, you are in the box and you can't move anywhere
4. **(to) blend in:** (1) to take something and mix it with something else (2) to harmonize
5. **(to) butter someone up:** to flatter somebody a lot, lot of flattering in order to get something, to spread nice words all over the person, to say many nice things to the person (so the person would like you. Maybe the person would do something for you)
6. **(to) butt out:** get out of here, mind your own business, leave,
7. **(to) belt out a song:** to sing a song really powerfully and loudly,
8. **Bogged down:** to be overburdened work, super busy, so much work and almost you are dying.
9. **(to) bail on somebody:** to leave a person in a difficult situation,
10. **(to) bow out:** to quit something but by showing respect
11. **Brush up on something:** to refresh your knowledge,
12. **Count on somebody:** Rely on somebody, trust or believe on somebody,
13. **Count me in/out:** to include somebody/something or to exclude somebody,

14. **Come down with:** getting sick with something,

15. **(to) come in on:** In this expression "on" referring to days like Sunday, Monday or weekend and we don't use in month. We only use it for days, so somebody will say to you like this *"can you come in on Wednesday?"* Also we can use it for numbers like *"can you come in on 4th?"* We usually use this expression in appointment situation

16. **Creep me out:** if something creep me out. That means, it's disgusting; I don't want to see it. For example, Cockroaches creep me out.

17. **(to) crack someone up:** to make the person laugh,

18. **(to) catch up:** to go faster so that you reach the person in front of you

19. **Coming along:** progressing,

20. **(to) chime in:** to give idea or suggestion, (2) to interrupt

21. **(to be) chummy with:** to be very close, to be very nice with someone, have a very good friendly relationship with someone,

22. **Chance for/of:** probability

23. **Chance to:** opportunity

24. **(to) come around:** (1) to visit, (2) to agree to somebody after a lot of thinking and argument,

25. **(to) chomp on (into) SMT:** to eat and take a big bite of your food, (loud type of chewing)

26. **Cozying up to someone:** to be very friendly and nicely with someone for getting advantage

27. **(to) do away with (something):** to get rid of something,

28. **(to) do (something) up:** to make something very special,

29. **(to) do up (something):** zip up something (clothes)

30. **(to) do it over:** to do it again,

31. **(to) die for:** really excellent, (2) to have strongly wish for something

32. **(to) dress up:** to wear your best cloths and look really good

33. **(to) dwell on something:** to constantly be thinking or talking about one thing,

34. **(to) dump on someone:** to tell somebody all of your problems, worries, fears, emotional thought and everything

35. **(to) dump something out!** to overturn, to spill something, to empty something, to throw something away,

36. **(to) dabble in:** to explore, to do a little bit not professionally,

37. **(to) drop off(verb) and drop-off(noun):** to put something at someplace, to leave something at somewhere,

38. **(to be) dense about something:** to be stupid, to not have knowledge about something

39. **(to) dole out:** to give something (a little)

40. **(to) dish out:** (1) to punish somebody, (2) to criticize somebody,

41. **Dead on:** perfectly accurate and right,

42. **Dying to do something:** super excited to do something,

43. **(to) dote on somebody:** to treat somebody very nicely, overly nicely,

44. **(to) fool around:** to be doing something that is not very important, to play (2) try to fix something,

45. **(to be) fresh out of something:** to not have anything, to have zero

46. **(to) fill somebody in:** to give someone important information (information that they are waiting for)

47. **(to) follow along:** to listen carefully so that you can understand,

48. **Go all out:** to do something with all your energy, passion and ability, do everything that you can do

49. **Go down...** to go to urban area, to go to town/hill, to go south side

50. **Goof off:** to play, to have a good time, to do nothing, to joke around, to tease each other,

51. **(To) get carried away:** to lose self-control while describing something, to get overexcited, go too far, to lose sense of proportion,

52. **(to) get through (Time):** to survive a period of time,

53. **(to) gloss over something:** to give just a little bit information not in depth or in detail.

54. **Hit someone up:** ask someone for something,

55. **(To) hang out:** to meet your friend and do nothing

56. **(to) hit on someone:** flirting with someone, seduce,

57. **Hit it off:** To get along very well, to become close friend,

58. **Hang it up:** to quit something,

59. **(to) iron out:** to solve problem

60. **(to) knock yourself out:** to exhaust yourself doing something

61. **(to) Kick off:** to start something,

62. **(To) look away:** Avert one's gaze

63. **(to) lose sleep over something:** To worry about something a lot

64. **(to) luck out:** to be lucky,

65. **(to) level up:** to improve, to go up to a higher level

66. **(to) mull something over:** to think about something

67. **(to) move up:** next level,

68. **Make it through:** to do something successfully, to arrive at the end of something safely, to recovered, to overcome some sort of difficulty,

69. **(to) make up (for):** to compensate something, (2) to create or compose something, (3) to reconcile, fixing the relationship,

70. **(to) nosh on something:** to snack on something, to nibble something

71. **(to) Put up with:** to endure,

72. **(to) Pig out:** to eat a lot like a pig.

73. **(to) pay it forward:** to pay for next person

74. **(to) put somebody on:** to hire someone,

75. **(to) pan out:** to become successful, to find success

76. **Plug in:** to fit something in; (2) to add something especially schedule;

77. **(to) pick it up:** (1)to pick something like pen/marker, (2)to clean like your room, (3)go faster, increase your speed,

78. **(to) patch things up:** to resolve a problem especially in relationship,

79. **(to) plug away:** to do something bit by bit, step by step, a little bit

80. **(to) quibble over:** to argue about something unimportant,

81. **(to) rile somebody up:** to get someone excited (negative meaning), to get someone angry

82. **(to) root for someone (common in sports):** to cheer for someone,

83. **(to) rustle up something:** to find or make something useful (but to find something is not easy)

84. **(to) rant about something:** to complain about something continually (maybe 10 or 30 minutes complain),

85. **to stock up on something:** to buy a lot of something, to buy huge amount of something

86. **To sell someone out:** to betray someone

87. **(to) straighten out:** to fix the problem, to resolve the problem

88. **Straight from...** directly from

89. **Slacking off:** to not do your work and do something else, to be lazy for a short time (not for long time)

90. **Slack up on somebody:** to be nicer and don't be so hard

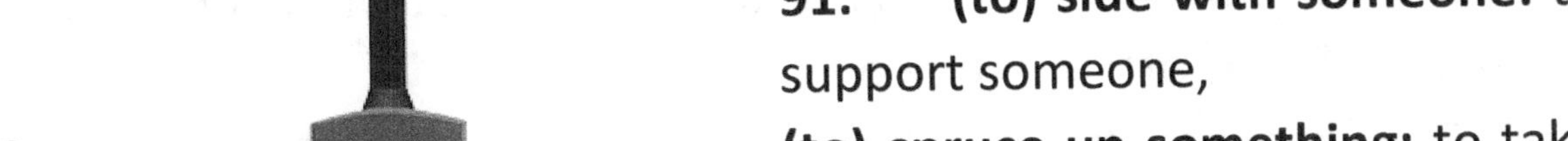

91. **(to) side with someone:** to support someone,

(to) spruce up something: to take something old and make it new,

(to) shell out: to spend a lot of money,

92.

93.

94. **Sleep on it:** to let the decision/answer come to you in few days later

95. **To stomp on / to stamp on:** While listening to the music, sometimes, you lightly hit your foot on the floor continually. That's the stamp on. You are stamping on he floor. Another example, if you throw the cigarette and you want to stamp on the cigarette. 'To stamp on something' and 'to stomp on something' have same meaning ut slightly different. 'To stomp on' is one-time heavy hit. And 'to stamp on' is light.

96.   **Step on:** For example, you are walking. And there is cell phone in the ground. Your foot unintentionally goes on the cell phone, and it breaks. In that situation, you can say *"I stepped on it."*

97.   **(to) turn in:** (1) to give something to somebody who asked for it (2) to go to the bed

98.   **(to) turn out:** to have a result

99.   **(to) Tinker around:** To fix and adjust something, to touch and check something,

100.   **To have someone over:** invite somebody in your house

101.   **Top it off:** to fill it completely,

102.   **(to) tough it out:** be tough and endure in difficult situation,

103.   **(to) take it out on somebody:** if your boss or teacher makes you angry, then you can't yell at your boss or teacher. So your anger and frustration are inside. And you go to your home and angry or yell at your mom, dad, sister or brother without any reason. So you took it out on your brother/sister. That's' the idea.

104.   **(to) tide someone over:** to give a person something to survive,

105.   **(to be) tied up with something:** to be busy with something

106.   **Ticked off:** to make someone really angry not exploding but frustrating,

107.   **(to) tear around / through:** to run really fast,

108.   **(to) tie one on:** to drink a lot alcohol,

109.   **take up with someone:** to become friends with someone; to become acquaintance with someone.

110.   **Take something up with someone:** to discuss something with someone to get advice or opinion.

111.   **take up (time):**, to eat time, to use time,

112.   **Take up something:** to study some subject like history, math etc...

113.   **(to) trip Someone out:** to shock somebody, (2) to make somebody angry or crazy,

114.   **(to) tap into something:** to go into something that's difficult to go into and take out the important stuff,

115.   **(to) trudge through:** (1) walk through sand, wet ground, or snow (2) to do a boring and hard work

116.   **(to be) up to something:** to be making an evil plan, to be doing something suspicious or secretly,

117.   **(to be) washed up:** not good anymore, no longer have talent,

118.   **(to) weasel out of something:** If somebody gives you some responsibility, work, or job, and you agree to do that. But in the last moment, you find some stupid excuse. Because, you don't want to do extra work. You love your friend, but you don't want to do work or help to your friend. This is the weaseling out of something.

119.   **To wear out:** exhaust, get tired through overuse, great strain, or stress

Bonus Section

Phrasal verbs with Give

1. **Give off:** to produce something like smell, heat or light.
2. **Give up:** to quit some work because of difficulty before you've finished it, accept defeat,
3. **Give and take:** mutual compromises, willing to exchange ideas with each other,
4. **Give oneself air:** to think and act in a way that shows one is better than others,
5. **Give chase**: to follow somebody for catching him,
6. **Give away:** give your things to somebody rather than selling
7. **Give in:** admit defeat after long time,
8. **Give way:** break down, (2) stop operating something,
9. **Give out:** Stop working,
10. **Give onto something**: to lead to some place,

Phrasal verbs with Get:

1. **Get back:** to return to a place,
2. **Get through:** Get success in making someone understand something
3. **Get off something:** to leave bus or train,
4. **Get down:** depress,
5. **Get up:** wake up, leave bed,
6. **Get at someone:** repeatedly criticize someone,
7. **Get about:** start walking

Phrasal verbs with Put:

1. **Put off:** to postpone,
2. **Put up with:** tolerate,
3. **Put down:** suppress a rebellion
4. **Put on:** to dress,
5. **Put by:** to save money for later use,

Phrasal verbs with Take:

1. **Take after someone:** to resemble,
2. **Take something back:** return something to the store
3. **Take down:** write something on the paper
4. **Take somebody in:** allow someone to stay at your home
5. **Take off:** depart hurriedly, (2) aero plane leave the ground
6. **Take something off:** to remove some clothes like shoes, socks,
7. **Take something on:** accept responsibility,
8. **Take someone on:** hire someone,
9. **Take over something:** to take control
10. **Take up something:** Fill time or space,

Phrasal verbs with Look:

1. **Look after:** to take care of someone/something
2. **Look ahead:** to think about (plan)
3. **Look back:** to think about past
4. **Look up:** search for something (especially in book)
5. **Look up to:** to admire somebody,

WORDS

01 - Already

Sometimes, we add the word 'already' at the end of the sentence. For example, "hurry up already"

Hurry up means 'do something quickly'. But when we add adverb 'already', it means that you should already have done it or you should already have started it. So 'hurry up already' is emphasizing you to hurry up.

Let me give you two examples, so you would understand that.

Your friend is late and he should be here by now, so you will call and say to him "where are you already".

In another situation;

You have only 5 minute remaining to complete a report and your boss will say to "you should do this already."

02 - Ad hoc:

Ad hoc is actually Latin for 'for this' and we use this word to describe the meeting, organization, community etc…like

Ad hoc meeting; ad hoc organization, ad hoc community.

And it means 'organization for this; community for this; meeting for this'. And what is 'this'?' 'This' is something temporarily but urgent. Government and business use this expression.

For example, a few years ago, in America there was a big tragedy at school called sandy hooks and many children were shot and killed by some young boy. So that was a big tragedy. And in America, a lot of schools made ad hoc community to discuss school security; how can they improve their school security. So these meetings were temporary, they don't go too long; maybe a couple months or maybe a year most and they are supposed to solve the issue. So it's not a permanent organization; it's temporary community for a special purpose.

03 – AWOL: Absent without leave (military expression), absent without permission,

04 - Auspicious (day, occasion, event, number):

Favorable, auguring favorable circumstances and good luck

05 - Average Joe: Just a regular guy nothing special,

06 - Aw, shucks!

We use this when we are embarrass; or when we want to show modesty; or when we are little bit humble.

For example, if somebody say to me "hay, Nabeel, you are so handsome."

"Aw, shucks! I am not that handsome." I would say that (showing modesty)

07 – Actionable: Something you can do,

08 – Apathy:

To not care about something, absence of enthusiasm or absence of interest in something

09 - A 2fer: 2 things for the price of 1, buy 1 get 1 free,

10 - 24/7: everyday,

11 – Asking: what is price?

12 – Brouhaha: fight between many people (not just two people)

13 - Black sheep: strange person, bad person

14 - Bah! Humbug! nonsense, ridicules, who cares,

15 – Bossy: like a boss, person who love to   tell somebody what to do,

16 - Bad omen: bad sign

17 - Bug (bugs) problem

18 - Bug (Health related) virus

19 – Blah: No good,

20 – Buff: heavy good solid muscle especially arms

21 – Bacon: money (especially job salary)

22 - Bug zapper: bug killer gadget (for killing mosquitoes, flies etc..)

23 – Bleak: unpleasantly cold, (2) no hope

24 - Bunny boiler: Bunny boiler refers to a woman who get really angry after breakup of her husband or boyfriend. A Boyfriend who cheated her.

25 - Brick and mortar: real and physical location or store,

26 - A bang-up job: to do a fantastic job

27 - Bass ackwards: (180 degree) opposite wrong way

28 – CONtent: written material inside

29 – content: happy and satisfy

30 – classic is adjective and it describe something typical; high quality

31 – Classical: it refer to classical music or art; very traditional, very ancient.

32 - Cheat sheet: cheat paper

33 – Corny: silly, childish, something is kind of stupid

34 – Crock: nonsense; not true; (for example, this website is crock)

35 – Crook: somebody who steal something without thinking,

36 – Crucial: extremely important,

37 – Chintzy: cheap, like a miser, scrooge,

38 - Chitchat VS shoot the breeze: to have a causal conversation not a deep conversation,

39 – Crabby: in bad mood,

40 – Cinch: really easy and simple,

40 - Can-do attitude: positive attitude,

41 - Corporate material: A person who might be able to become a leader of the company,

42 – Cowlick: bad and messy hair (after the wake up)

43 - Chronic pain: pain that never goes away,

44 – Cockamamie: ridicules, stupid (ideas)

45 - A close shave: a very smooth clean shave,

46 - A crackpot idea: a stupid idea,

47 - Crocodile tears: fake tears,

47 - Complete wash: complete waste (money, time etc.)

47 - Close call: a narrow escape from difficult situation, a barely successful escape,

48 - A charley horse: if you are running fast, and then suddenly, your leg hit a table. It is so painful and you can't move. Than you can say, you have a charley horse.

In the football game, some player try to hit your leg, so they give you a charley horse.

49 - A cakewalk: Very easy

50 - The consensus: General agreement (what the majority of people say or want),

51 – Cushy: Nice and pleasant job without any stress,

52 – Devastated: very sad, destroyed (very series expression)

53 - Dirt poor: to have no money

54 – Dump: place where you throw garbage (located in outside the city), trash,

55 – Dumpster: really large trashcan

56 - Duh--! of course, why did you ask?

56 - A dope: a stupid person,

56 - (To be) dope: really cool/good

57 – Dork: a weird and silly person,

57 - Drain: deprive the energy/strength

58 - day job! regular job, main job

59 – Drag: extremely boring,

60 – Doughboy: fat guy,

61 – Dumbstruck: amazed and shocked,

62 - Double whammy: double attack, attack from two different places,

63 - Diddly squat: nothing,

64 – Drivel: stupid words

65 - Drama queen: a person who reacts too emotionally in situations, person who overreact,

66 - Dead broke: to really have no money, zero money,

67 - Even (verb): 'even' is used to empathize something amazing or surprising

68 - Elbow grease: elbow power

69 – Earnest: really hardworking person,

70 – Frazzled: confused, stressed, worried,

71 – Freebies: free things that you receive when you go to the store and buy something

72 – Flickering: lights that is about to dead, a momentary flash of light

73 - Farm-to-fork: foods that is produced in local farm and immediately goes to the restaurant or in your kitchen,

74 – Freeloader: person who loves the free stuff,

75 – Flimsy: very thin and insubstantial, week argument,

76 – Flabbergasted: shocked, astonished,

77 – Flab: fat,

78 – Fickle: person who changes their mind, heart, or feelings for no reason.

79 – Floored: to be completely shocked,

80 - Fat chance / slim chance: tiny chance, low probability,

81 – Grueling: exhausting,

82 – Grand: a thousand (dollars)

83 – Gibberish: nonsense,

84 – Goosebumps: we use this in especially two situations; when we are cold, and when we are scared *"oh, I have Goosebumps"*

85 - Holidays, vacation and weekend

Holidays are the red number in a calendar like Christmas, New Year or sometimes Valentine's Day.

And when we say vacations, then it means, a period of time when we don't have to work like summer vacation or sometimes three days' vacation. And finally word, weekend refers to Saturday or Sunday.

86 – Hone: to sharpen,

86 - Great taste: high quality things or best things

87 - Hoopla: lots of excitement or talking,

88 - High-profile: Opposite of low-key

89 - Head honcho: the boss

90 - Holiday cheer: holiday happiness,

91 – Hodgepodge: a confusing mixture of this & that

92 – Heading: going

93 - A hollow victory: empty victory, bad victory,

94 – Highbrow: highly cultured or educated, a person of intellectual or erudite tastes,

95 – Hubris: too much confidence

96 - Hand-me-downs

hand-me-downs is usually clothing that your elder brother or elder sister wore.

Many times, your mom doesn't buy you a new cloth. She gives you clothes that your elder brother used.

Your elder brother is too big, so now you have to wear it.

97 - Hot-button issue: very controversial topic,

98 - Home wrecker: a person/something who cause to breaks up the relationship,

99 – INTENS: in an extreme degree, extremely sharp or intense, very strong and powerful feeling,

100 – Industrious: hard working

101 – Inscribe: carve, cut, or etch into a material or surface,

102 - An invigorating sleep: wonderful sleep, totally rested, very relax,

103 – Iffy: if you are not sure about something, you can't say 'yes'; and you can't say 'No'. That's iffy.

104 - A jerk: a selfish guy who only think about himself, a mean person

105 - A jock: a physically healthy and fit person who loves sports and exercise;

106 - Jealousy VS envy

If someone is better than you... For example, if a person have better English pronunciation skills, and you wish that you had it, so you envy that person. But jealousy is that... For example, you have two friends; friend A and Friend B. And friend A like friend B more than you. So you are jealous.

So idea is that, envy is between two peoples and jealousy is between three peoples. So if someone is successful and you are not, that is envy. And jealousy requires a person that you might lose.

107 – Junkie: heroine addicted person,

108 – Kowtow: to give someone too much respect; to be so nice

109 – Kerfuffle: some craziness, a commotion, argument,

110 - A knee-jerk reaction/response: automatically, without thinking,

111- A knee-slapper: super funny,

112 - A knuckle dragger: a scary and big guy like an animal (gorilla)

113 – Knack: ability

114 - Low-key

Low key is used to describe colors. Brown or dark are low-key color but white or yellow is not low-key colors.

Also, this expression is used to describe people. Some peoples are very bright, talkative, very active and they have lots of fun. So these people are not low-key. And some people are very calm and pretty quiet. Those are low-key peoples.

115 - Litterbugs

people who throw anywhere their trash (like piece of paper) called litterbugs

116 - A loose cannon

it describe somebody who gets angry very easily and punches you or yell it you

117 - Leftovers

The food that you had the dinner/lunch, but you didn't finish all of the food. And you can throw away the food, or you can keep the food and put into the refrigerator; and later you can eat them. That's food is the leftovers.

118 - Like-minded: to think similar, to have same opinions

118 - (to be) long-winded: somebody who talks a lot

119 - A longshot: unlikely happening, probably it won't happen,

120 - Lemming, sheep, sheeple: mindless person called lemming, sheep or sheeple

121 - The lowdown: real important fundamental information but not necessary

122 - A loud tie: too bright color of something,

123 - A living legend

Somebody who has done something amazing, (so every person respects him), true leader in one area,

124 – Leeway: freedom

125 - Lowest common denominator:

Regular person (low iq people; opposite of intellectual person)

126 - Live wire

A person who is super full of energy (emotionally and physical movement just like a electricity live wire)

127 - Light wallet: to not have lot of money,

128 - Monkey business

<u>Meaning:</u> (1) something that is waste of time, something silly, (2) something immoral or illegal

<u>Explanation:</u> if you are playing online gambling games in your company; that is monkey business.

So something that is not too series, you are not going to jail. This is monkey business

129 - May be OR maybe

maybe is adverb and it means perhaps; **may be** = might be

130 - A mooch: a mooch is a person who takes your things without asking

131 - Minute (not about time!): very small

132 - Midnight snack

If you are sleeping at night and at midnight, you awake suddenly and you feel hungry, then you go to the kitchen and start eating something. That's the midnight snack.

133 – Mental: stupid

134 - Moo juice: Milk

135 - Murphy's Law

<u>Meaning:</u> anything that can go wrong with

<u>Explanation:</u> You have planned for and it's going to be perfect but suddenly, something happened and complete destruction. It's Murphy's Law.

You have planned to do this, and something will destroy your plan.

136 - Monday-morning quarterback

<u>Meaning:</u> to tell someone what they should have do after the mistake

<u>Explanation</u>: If your friend make a mistake, and after his mistake and his failure, you tell him that he made a mistake. Also you tell him what he should have do. But now you are telling your friend his mistake, and it doesn't help him. You should already told him. Now he have made a mistake, so he knows his mistake; he had known what he should do. So your advice doesn't help him. In that situation, we can say that you are

being Monday morning quarterback. Monday morning quarterback bother other person.

137 - The mother lode: large amount of something,

138 - The Midas touch

if somebody has Midas touch in something, that means, they have special power or ability to make something successful. For example, she has Midas touch in cooking. That means, whatever she cooks, it taste delicious.

139 - 9 out of 10 times: 90%

140 - Nuance: meaning (message in the words)

141 - Nasty: mean, not nice, dirty, very bad,

142 - Nagging: to annoy someone by repetitive complain or questions

143 - A nail-biter: a game/movie situation that make you really nerves scared or anxious because ending is unknown,

144 - A no-brainer: obvious,

145 - The nitty-gritty: very specific information, important and particular information about the subject,

146 - Nauseous: to feel sick in your stomach like vomit,

147 - No-nonsense: Simple, straightforward, logical, nothing silly and confusing, easy,

148 - Nightcap: final drink of the evening, (relaxing drink)

149 - One too many: too much

150 - Out of date: old fashioned,

151 - An old-timer: for a longtime, (2) if someone is lot of experience in one area, is called an old-timer

152 – Pathetic: something that lacks ability, something is terrible and ridicules, inadequate,

153 - Pouting

a little bit angry; make a sad face and thrust out one's lower lip; be in a huff and display one's displeasure.

154 – perplexed: Very confused

155 - Per se: in itself, as such

156 - Pizzazz : give something extra excitement, make extra special

157 - A poor excuse: lie, bad excuse,

158 – Peachy: great,

159 – Peddling: to sell something, sell or offer for sale from place to place

160 - PERIOD!

I have nothing more to say,

for example I love writing books PERIOD!

161 – Piecemeal: piece by piece, bit by bit, one step at a time, slowly, gradually,

162 – Pesky: causing irritation or annoyance, something that bothers you like bugs

163 – Painstaking: hard work (kind of stressful)

164 – Pirating: to takes something that doesn't belong to you and then sell it to other people,

165 - (to be) pumped: very excited, full of energy and power, ready to go and do something,

166 - Potluck

<u>Explanation</u>: In America, sometimes there is party in school, church or other place. In that party, you have to bring some food. This is called potluck dinner, potluck party or potluck lunch. You have to make some food at home, and take it in that party.

167 - (to) pledge: to promise with deep emotions inside

168 – Pooped: tired, exhausted, energy is gone,

169 - Roly-poly: nice and bouncy fat, round fat

170 - R.I.P. (Rest in Peace): we use this expression, when somebody dies. It shows respect.

171 – Retrospective: an exhibition of a representative selection of an artist's life work

172 - The refs: referee.

173 - Rat's nest: messy,

174 - A rubbernecker: distracted,

175 - The runs

it means, your stomach is not feeling well and you need to go to the bathroom. You can say "I've got the runs."

176 - A rain check: a ticket given for later use

177 – Ruse: deception, trick,

178 - Rats!

We say this word, when something bad happened. For example, *"Oh, I forgot my wallet. Rats!"*

179 – RSVP: response please,

180 - Razzle-dazzle

some sort of decoration or feature that is very exciting, bright and very colorful,

181 - Red-eye flight

normally, you take a flight in daytime and arrive at any destination in day time. But red-eye flight leaves very late at night and arrives at the destination early in the morning.

182 - A red letter day: special and important day,

183 - (to) riff

to talk about something without any planning, just talking, discuss very casually,

184 - A sneezing fit: Nonstop sneezing, continue to sneeze

185 - Sooner or later: Eventually; within an indefinite time or at an unspecified future time

186 - (to be) Slick! a slippery smoothness,

When we say he is slick, it means he can go anywhere and cause a problem and he never have a problem. He is like a snack.

187 - Sneak attack: to attack somebody in a surprising way (quiet manner)

188 - Sweet tooth

I have a sweet tooth and it means, I like to eat sweet things like candy, cake, ice-cream anything sweet.

189 - Smooth sailing: no trouble and no problem, everything is nice

Are your life smooth sailing? Is your relationship is smooth sailing?

190 - Shady guy

somebody who is sneaky, thief like a snack, somebody that you can't really trust and somebody who is strange and you don't like

191 - A shadow: Black outline that you see when the light shine at something

192 - (to) shadow: to follow somebody

193 – Swagger: to walk with a lofty proud gait, often in an attempt to impress others

194 - Squirt

some time you peel the orange, its squirt (*a little water come out and maybe come in your eyes),* splash

195 - Slacker

a person who shirks their work or duty (especially one who tries to evade military service in wartime)

196 - (to) scramble: to hurry, to quickly,

197 - A stroke of luck: by luck, by chance

198 - A stickler: someone who really sticks to the rule; person who follow the rules precisely,

199 - A stepping stone: something that help to get the goal/target/destination

200 – Steep: a steep place (as on a hill) (2) much more expensive

201 – Snubbed: to be ignore especially in that situation where you deserve appreciation.

202 - (to) swerve: To turn quickly and suddenly

Explanation: when we are driving fast, we move our car left or right quickly, that's movement is swerve

203 - A Sunday driver

Explanation: Sunday driver are those people who drive car very slowly; they don't have any emergency; they enjoy nature and go slowly.

204 - A sticky situation: situation that is very hard to handle/manage; very uncomfortable,

205 – Savvy: to be smart, to understand, ability to make good judgment,

206 - Slow jam: slow and romantic music

207 - A slew of something: a lot of something, a huge amount of something

208 - (to be) stoked: excited, very enthusiastic,

209 - Sob VS wail VS whimper

sob: very wet cry (little kids cry like this),

Wail: cry very loudly,

Whimper: (animals or girlfriend are the example of the whimper crying

210 – Sugarcoat: lie, being nice,

211 – Snazzy: looks really nice, special and cool

212 - Second to none: the best,

213 - STILL!

Meaning: anyway, (2) you have to,

Explanation: For example, a small boy gets small piece of cake on his birthday and he want more; so he says to his mom *"I need more cake"*,

Mom says *"no, it's not good for your health"*

Boy says *"STILL!"* That means 'anyway', I need more cake.

214 – Scatterbrain: person who is unable to concentrate,

215 - Shoot! Go ahead, ask your question, say it,

216 - Spoiler alert: where someone gives away the main plot or turning point in a movie

217 – Sheer: clear, absolutely, pure, completely,

218 - Silver bullet: solution,

219 - A stand-up guy: a respectable person, very good and ethical guy,

220 – Swanky: really nice, luxurious (probably expensive)

221 - Snake oil: something that is not medically proved, lie (just marketing)

Explanation: The medicines, that are fake, can be called snake oil.

222 - (to be) a slam-dunk: to be amazingly successful,

223 - Stick-to-itiveness: determination, dedication, persistent,

224 - Smooth move

Explanation: if you try to do something, and it really works perfectly, that's the smooth move. But we also use this sarcastically.

225 - A Scrooge, a tightwad: A person who has lot of money but they don't want to spend it,

226 - A sad state of affairs: dismal situation and circumstances, (like economy, political, environmental etc...)

227 - A typo: A typing mistake like spelling or punctuation mistake

228 - Tar baby: problem that would stick with you; you can't rid of this

229 – Tops: (1) the best (2) no more than

230 - Trip VS travel VS journey

Meaning: travel is a verb, trip is a noun.

And a trip is a short journey. Journey is a long vacation or a long trip

231 - Twoosh!

Meaning: for only twitter user – perfect message of 140 characters, (because twitter limit is 140 characters you don't write more)

Explanation: you are thinking in your mind and then start type message in twitter without think about the character and when you done; it's a 140 character typed in twitter, then you would say "twoosh" That means perfect.

232 – Trendy: popular, (like trendy music; trendy shopping mall)

233 - A train wreck: we use this to describe a person. He is a train wreck and it means he is a disaster.

234 - (to be) thick-skinned

<u>**Explanation:**</u> if somebody is thick-skinned, that means this person is not emotional when other people criticize him; they don't get angry or mad.

235 - top shelf: best

236 - (to) tank: to run out of, to become empty, to be depleted

237 - Two-faced: two personality,

238 - Thrift shop: shop where you can buy really cheap used clothes, toys and anything used,

239 – Telemarketers: somebody who trying to sell something and talk to you in great detail,

240 – Tight: close friend, best friend forever,

241 – Tupperware: any type of container that you can put food into,

242 – Tenacity: determination, not giving up,

243 – TP: toilet paper,

244 - (to) touch base: Reestablish relationship,

245 - Thingamajig

<u>**Explanation**</u>: we use the word 'thingamajig' when we don't know the name of the thing. Memorize this word. Because, there are many nouns to memorize in English. If you can't memorize all the name, you can just use this word.

246 - Trade-off: bad part,

247 - A tab

<u>**Explanation**</u>: That means, you are going to order some food or drinks at the restaurant, but you are not going to pay now. After you finish, you

may order more and you are going to pay. After the end of the night, you are going to pay. So in this situation, when you go to the restaurant, you can ask *"can I start a tab?"*

248 – Urbanite: opposite of dork, person who love city and attractive style,

249 – Veggies: vegetables.

250 – Willpower: strengthen of mind, determination, power and ability to make the decision

251 - Writer's block: the condition of being unable to think of what to write,

252 - Weather VS climate: weather is short term but climate is a long term

253 – Wherewithal: money

254 – Whatsoever:

<u>Explanation</u>: It emphasizes words; none, no one, anyone etc... For example; none at all; anyone at all etc...

I have nothing whatsoever. It means, I have nothing at all.

255 - Weed (marijuana, dope, grass, pot): a drug

256 - Wishy-washy: feel difficulty to make decision,

THE END